SWEET AND SAVORY COOKBOOK

BY GWEN KENNEALLY

ILLUSTRATED BY ALEXANDRA CONN

Copyright 2011 by Huqua Press
An operating unit of Morling Manor Corporation

ISBN 978-0-9838120-1-2

First published in 2011 by Huqua Press
Los Angeles, California

Cover and text design by Alexandra Conn

No part of this book may be reproduced or transmitted in any form
by any means without permission from the author or publisher.

huquapress.com

Printed in the United States of America

To my awesome and beautiful daughter, Emma Rose.

Thank you for choosing me to be your mom. You make the great joys of life so much sweeter and you give me the strength and courage to move through the savory times.

FOREWORD

There's magic in movie making, just like there's magic in the kitchen. The more detailed and authentic or surprising a film is, the more it connects with an audience. Food is the same way, and Gwen Kenneally is truly the master of bringing heart and spirit to her cooking.

Whenever I host a fund-raiser or party at our home, be it for Hillary Clinton or the Baker's Dozen of Yale, Gwen is on hand, serving some of my favorites: coconut shrimp, crab cakes, turkey burgers with cranberries and ginger and Crème Brulee French Toast. (She even renamed her signature breakfast dish Cream Beauty French Toast to commemorate our Oscar win for American Beauty. Nice touch, Gwen). She's always brought love and joy to her food, and now she brings the same to this, her first collection of recipes.

Hollywood often is drawn to cutting edge trends and the shiny and new. Sweet and Savory may be new to the palates of some, but Gwen's been mixing it up for years, and has been delivering the goods long before agave and ginger had each other at hello.

- Bruce Cohen

INTRODUCTION

A sweet and savory aroma warmly drifts from the kitchen into the living room where my guests are gathered. Their taste buds tingle in anticipation of the gastro delight that awaits. Is it dinner? Is it dessert? They can't quite define the temptation, they only know it smells pretty wonderful — and they are eager for that first magical bite.

The dictionary says of sweet: Having the taste of sugar or a substance containing or resembling cane sugar, as honey or agave. Pleasant to the palate. And of savory: Piquant, pungent, or salty to the taste; not sweet yet pleasant.

The notion of sweet and savory isn't new (a popular chocolate candy has been betrothed to peanut butter for years, after all). A century ago frugal cooks mixed up leftovers with whatever they found in their kitchens, often resulting in culinary discoveries such as learning that sauerkraut mixed in cake batter made a moister cake — with a savory edge. Now, like never before, the savory/sweet combo is taking the food world by storm. Who would have thought that bacon would find its way to cupcakes, ice cream, chocolate bars, or even tucked inside pancake batter, with such ferocity – other than perhaps as a dare or college prank.

Today, the saltier, the brinier, the sweeter, the stickier — the better. The culinary landscape has become a place of art, adventure and a bit of science—with flavors taking on bold identities, mandating that alternating flavors complement each other.

As a Hollywood chef and caterer, my clients expect me to not only keep up with culinary trends; they rely on me to pave the way. They also know I embrace family recipes, comfort foods and diversity in my menu planning. What they might not know is that sweet and savory has been part of my repertoire for decades now.

When my daughter was a baby I made all of her food and was inspired to add a little cinnamon to her carrots or a pinch of ginger to her sweet potatoes. As a child, she would ask for green pasta (pesto) and pink chicken (salmon). As her palate expanded (and demanded), so would mine.

INTRODUCTION

This collection of sweet and savory recipes contains many of the dishes I serve to clients, friends and family —from holidays to Hollywood parties and political events.

Some of my favorite sweet and savory recipes came to be by necessity, some by tireless experimentation and others with a fanciful desire to create something fresh and interesting. The Strawberry Margarita pie was a Cinco de Mayo inspiration. Since I began my week-end cocktail column I have been besieged with requests for the latest and greatest martini and have included some of those in this collection, including my signature Spa Cocktail. And the Shirley Temple Scone was created just for this cookbook. Friends, family and even my daughter have contributed to many of these recipes, and I invite you to add a pinch of whatever here or there to make them your own.

So grab some ginger, rosemary, orange zest, agave and cinnamon, your epicurean sense of adventure and join me in the kitchen for a journey to the land of sweet and savory, won't you?

- Gwen Kenneally

TABLE OF CONTENTS

FOREWORD

INTRODUCTION

APPETIZERS

9 ROASTED FIGS AND MAYTAG BLUE CHEESE

10 SHRIMP AND CACTUS PEAR COCKTAIL

10 FRESH FIG SALSA

11 PEACH GINGER MINT SALSA

11 PINEAPPLE, JICAMA AND THAI CHILI SALSA

12 STRAWBERRY SALSA

12 WATERMELON SALSA

13 POMEGRANATE GUACAMOLE

14 HOMEMADE TORTILLA CHIPS

15 SHRIMP WITH COCONUT

16 VEGETARIAN MOON ROLLS

17 DIPPING SAUCE

17 PROSCIUTTO WITH MELON

SOUPS

18 THAI CHICKEN AND COCONUT SOUP

19 PEAR AND BUTTERNUT SQUASH SOUP

20 AVGOLEMONO (GREEK LEMON SOUP)

21 CREAMY WINTER SQUASH & APPLE SOUP

22 PUMPKIN AND GRUYERE SOUP

23 CARROT ORANGE GINGER SOUP

SALADS & SIDES

24 POMEGRANATE, BEETS, FENNEL & BLOOD ORANGE SALAD

25 MIXED GREENS WITH PEARS, GORGONZOLA AND MAPLE SYRUP VINAIGRETTE

26 CLEMENTINE CAESAR SALAD

27 SWEET POTATO SALAD

28 CITRUS RICE SALAD

29 CORN MAQUE CHOUX

30 BUTTERNUT SQUASH IN COCONUT MILK

31 BLACK BEAN & RED PAPAYA SALAD

32 POMEGRANATE AND QUINCE CHICKEN SALAD

33 CURRIED LOBSTER AND MANGO SALAD

34 SHRIMP AND BERRY SALAD WITH CITRUS VINAIGRETTE

35 SPINACH SALAD WITH BAKED GOAT CHEESE, PEARS AND DRIED CHERRIES

36 GRILLED SALMON AND STARFRUIT SALAD

37 MINT SOBA NOODLES

37 WATERMELON AND MANGO WITH LIMES AND MINT

MAINS

38 ROAST CHICKEN WITH PEAR

39 CRANBERRY CHICKEN

40 LIME TARRAGON CHICKEN

41 PECAN PEACH CHICKEN

42 GRILLED KEY LIME CHICKEN WITH BLACK BEAN SAUCE

43 APRICOT AND MAYTAG BLUE CHEESE STUFFED CHICKEN

43 BLOOD ORANGE BARBECUED CHICKEN

44 FIG AND ORANGE CHICKEN

45 TURKEY BURGER WITH CRANBERRIES AND GINGER

46 ORANGE AND VEGETABLE KABOB

47 GRILLED SHRIMP AND GINGER LIME MARINADE

48 ROASTED SALMON WITH POMEGRANATE AND AVOCADO

TABLE OF CONTENTS

49 CHILEAN SEA BASS WITH CRANBERRY BUTTER SAUCE
50 MAHI MAHI WITH BLOOD ORANGE SALSA
51 SWORDFISH WITH RED GRAPEFRUIT
52 GINGER SOY SALMON
53 GRILLED CHILEAN SEA BASS WITH WATERMELON SALSA
54 CAJUN SALMON WITH CHIPOTLE SQUASH AND MANGO SALSA
55 BRISKET WITH PORTOBELLO AND DRIED CRANBERRIES
56 GRILLED LAMB CHOPS WITH A SPICY MANGO SAUCE

PASTA & BREADS

57 PUMPKIN RISOTTO
58 FETTUCCINE WITH FIGS AND PANCETTA
59 LEMON CREAM FETTUCCINE
60 LEMON ROSEMARY RISOTTO
61 ROASTED GARLIC, CRANBERRY AND ROSEMARY BISCUITS
62 JALAPENO CORNBREAD
62 CRANBERRY-CHIPOTLE COMPOTE

DESSERTS

63 GREEN TEA AND CHOCOLATE TRUFFLES
64 PEAR TART WITH MAYTAG BLUE CHEESE CRUST
65 PECAN SWEET POTATO PIE
66 MIXED BERRY WITH LAVENDER SHORT CAKE
67 MEXICAN CHOCOLATE SOUFFLÉ WITH COFFEE SAUCE
68 24-KARAT CAKE
69 LEMON ROSEMARY POUND CAKE
70 CHOCOLATE BEET BUNDT CAKE
71 NONI'S RICOTTA PIE
72 CHOCOLATE AVOCADO CAKE
73 STRAWBERRY MARGARITA PIE

74 SHIRLEY TEMPLE SCONES
75 CHOCOLATE COVERED PRETZEL CHEESECAKE
75 CHOCOLATE COVERED PRETZELS

COCKTAILS

76 HOT CHERRY PEPPER MARTINI
76 JALAPEÑO MARGARITA
77 PEAR AND ROSEMARY MARTINI
78 GINGER INFUSED VODKA AND LEMONGRASS GREEN TEA
78 GINGER SYRUP
79 APPLE GINGER MARTINI
79 GWEN'S SPA COCKTAIL
79 SALTY DOG
80 THE LAVENDER MARTINI
81 CUCUMBER AND WATERMELON MOJITO
81 THE MINT JULEP
82 ROSEMARY LEMON MARTINI
83 LIMONCELLO
83 KASTEL PUMPKIN PUNCH

84 ACKNOWLEDGEMENTS

APPETIZERS

ROASTED FIGS AND MAYTAG BLUE CHEESE

Fig season is late summer and just a tidy four weeks here in Southern California. For years friends have dropped off bags of their surplus figs (it's either me or the squirrels!) and I know every August I'll be getting my fig on, creating thrilling new dishes with this curious little fruit. This is one of my favorite fig offerings. Pairing fresh figs with the Iowa cheese handmade by the appliance family since the early 1940's (yes, *that* Maytag) offers a richness, creaminess and tartness that I've not yet found in other types of blue cheese.

20 fresh black figs
1 cup Maytag blue cheese
¼ cup pecans, finely chopped
1 head of garlic
2 vanilla beans, split
8 ounces white balsamic vinegar
¼ cup sugar

Preheat oven to 375°. Wrap garlic with skin on and drizzle with olive oil in foil. Roast for one hour. Combine the balsamic, vanilla bean and sugar in a saucepan over medium heat and whisk continually until reduced to a thick glaze. Cool. Slice figs in half and set aside. Blend the blue cheese, pecans and garlic and place in a pastry bag. Pipe (or spoon) the blue cheese blend onto the fig halves. Heat the figs in pre-heated 375° oven for about five minutes then drizzle the balsamic glaze on the warm figs. Serve immediately. **Serves six.**

SHRIMP AND CACTUS PEAR COCKTAIL

2 pounds shrimp, steamed
3 cactus pears, chopped
1 large red onion, diced
1 red pepper, diced
1 cucumber
1 small jalapeno pepper, minced
1 sprig parsley, chopped
Juice of 3 limes
4 tablespoons grape seed or vegetable oil
Pinch salt and pepper

Ever so gently toss all ingredients. Chill overnight. Great served in an oversized martini or margarita glass. **Serves four**

FRESH FIG SALSA

2 cups (about 1 pound) fresh firm-ripe figs, stemmed and diced
2 mangos, diced
¼ cup very finely slivered fresh ginger
1 red onion, cut into thin slivers
1 to 2 small jalapeños, very thinly sliced
½ cup coarsely cut cilantro
Juice of 2-3 limes
Juice of 1 lemon
Salt to taste

Combine all ingredients and chill several hours to blend flavors. Serve with broiled or grilled fish, chicken, pork, beef or lamb. Or simply serve with chips for dipping. **Serves six.**

PEACH GINGER MINT SALSA

A friend with a tomato allergy inspired me to create tomato-less alternatives to enjoy the heat and flavor of salsa. This lively offering is a great accompaniment for chips but also nicely dresses chicken, fish or even Portobello mushrooms.

1 cup peaches, diced
1 cup cucumber, diced
¼ cup green onions, diced
2 teaspoons sugar
2 teaspoons cider vinegar
1 inch ginger, minced
Salt and pepper to taste

Combine all ingredients and stir well. Chill. **Serves six.**

PINEAPPLE, JICAMA AND THAI CHILI SALSA

The fire of Thai Chili is like no other, as it's a gentle heat. Paired with the sweetness of pineapple and the crunchiness of jicama, it makes for a dynamic salsa. Whenever I serve it at catered parties or at a gathering at home, friends and clients rave. And devour.

1 ½ cups pineapple, diced
1 ½ cups jicama, diced
Juice of 3 limes
½ cup fresh mint leaves, torn into small pieces
4 green onions, thinly sliced
1 teaspoon sugar
½ teaspoon kosher salt
4-10 Thai chilies, finely chopped

In a bowl, combine all the ingredients, cover with plastic wrap, and let stand for at least 1 hour at room temperature or for up to 8 hours refrigerated (the longer the flavors marry, the hotter the salsa will be). **Serves six.**

STRAWBERRY SALSA

Each year in Ventura County (just south of Santa Barbara) a mammoth Strawberry Festival takes place over the course of a May week-end. I sampled a strawberry salsa-like creation one year and it was tasty but needed a little something more. So I expanded upon it and created this version, which is especially incredible on sea bass, mahi mahi or pork. For a surprising treat on game day, have a bowl of taro chips on hand for dipping.

1 pint fresh strawberries, diced
4 roma tomatoes, seeded and chopped
1 jalapeño pepper, seeded and minced
4 cloves garlic, minced
1 lime, juiced
1 tablespoon olive oil

In a large bowl, combine strawberries, tomatoes, pepper, garlic, lime juice and oil. Toss all together to mix and coat. Cover dish and refrigerate for two hours to chill. **Serves six.**

WATERMELON SALSA

3 cups watermelon, chopped
½ cup green bell peppers, chopped
Juice of 1 lime
1 tablespoon chopped cilantro
1 tablespoon chopped green onion
1 tablespoon jalapeno peppers, chopped
(use up to 2 tablespoons chopped jalapenos, depending on taste and heat preference)
½ teaspoon garlic salt

Combine all ingredients. Cover and refrigerate 1 hour. **Serves six.**

POMEGRANATE GUACAMOLE

My daughter loves pomegranates and one Christmas I had an abundance of them and knew it was time to get creative in the kitchen. Given it was the holiday season I chose to pair the pomegranate with something green, and even though December isn't the optimum month for avocado enjoyment, somehow it all worked. In theory this recipe should serve six, but it typically disappears in moments and can be easily doubled or tripled to accommodate all of your guests.

2 large ripe avocados
1 red onion
3 garlic cloves
2 fresh jalapeños, seeded
2 tablespoons cilantro
Juice and zest of 2 limes
½ teaspoon salt
1 tablespoon pomegranate juice
3 tablespoons pomegranate seeds

Finely chop the onion, garlic, jalapeños, and cilantro. Place in bowl and add lime juice, zest and salt. Set aside. Peel and pit the avocados and place in a bowl. Mash with fork slowly, adding the tablespoon of pomegranate juice. Add onion and garlic mixture and fold together to make a course pulp. Gently fold in pomegranate seeds. Serve with warm tortillas, tostadas, or corn chips. **Serves four to six.**

HOMEMADE TORTILLA CHIPS

I know it's so much easier to toss a bag of store bought into your cart, but if you have even a few extra minutes, it's so worth it to make them from scratch. And we cheat a little with store bought tortillas, so there's really no excuse to at least give it a try.

Note: peanut oil is the best for holding heat. If you have a nut allergy try coconut oil or vegetable oil.

12 count package of corn tortillas
Peanut oil for frying
Kosher salt

Preheat oil in deep skillet. On a cutting board, stack four tortillas and cut into eight wedges. Repeat with remaining tortillas. Add a handful of wedges to the hot oil. Separate any that stick together. Fry until golden brown. Remove and drain on a cookie sheet lined with a brown paper bag or paper towels. Sprinkle with salt and continue with the remaining tortillas. **Serves four to six.**

SHRIMP WITH COCONUT

When I first started my catering business a client requested coconut shrimp for a milestone birthday party. It was not part of my catering menu, but I learned early on that when a client makes a request, I do what I can to make it happen. While experimenting in my kitchen, I pulled out a box of Trader Joe's pancake mix to use as a base for the batter. It was spectacular, puffy and golden. When I later made it with regular flour it just didn't have the same lightness or texture. So I only use pancake mix and this remains one of my most popular offerings.

3 pounds shrimp
3 cups shredded coconut (on a plate)
2 cups pancake mix
1 cup orange juice
½ cup coconut milk (more to thin the batter)
2 eggs
1 teaspoon cayenne pepper
Peanut oil for frying

Set deep fryer or wok for 375°. In a bowl mix pancake mix, eggs, orange juice, coconut milk and cayenne pepper. Holding by the tail, dip each shrimp into the batter, roll in the coconut and drop into bubbling oil. Do not overcrowd the fryer; cooking several batches as necessary. Fry until shrimp are golden brown; about three minutes. Do not overcook, as the shrimp gets tough. Drain on a brown bag. Serve hot. **Serves six.**

VEGETARIAN MOON ROLLS

My signature vegetarian dish began as a culinary disaster. I was catering an event in Malibu, nearly an hour away from my prep kitchen. Early on in my career I hadn't quite mastered the art of packing, and when my assistant and I showed up at the spectacular oceanfront estate I saw that the egg rolls the client had requested for her children had tumbled all over the van and were a hot mess. I dispatched my assistant to a nearby Chinese restaurant to persuade them to sell us egg roll wrappers, but they had none to spare and instead offered potsticker wrappers. Round instead of square, they were impossible to shape in the traditional fashion. So I created half moons and with less dough and more filling, a client favorite was born.

1 tablespoon olive oil
1 teaspoon sesame oil
Pinch of sea salt
1 cup carrots
1 each red and yellow bell peppers, halved and sliced
1 ½ cups snow peas, thinly sliced
1 cup green cabbage, chopped
2 cloves garlic
1 teaspoon fresh ginger

¼ cup fresh cilantro
2 teaspoons sake
2 teaspoons white wine vinegar
¼ cup vegetarian hoisin sauce
1 tablespoon chili sauce
1 package potsticker wrappers
1 egg, beaten
3 cups of peanut oil for cooking

Heat wok over high heat until very hot. Add sesame oil, olive oil and salt, then garlic and ginger. Cook for a minute and then add the vegetables and cook about six minutes, stirring frequently. Transfer to a bowl and add sake, rice vinegar, hoisin sauce, chili sauce and cilantro.

To make moon rolls, place 2 to 3 tablespoons of filling in the center of the wrapper. Using your fingers or a pastry brush spread egg all around the edges. Fold in half and pinch the edges tightly.

Heat three cups of peanut oil (substitute oil of your choice for guests with peanut allergies) on high heat. Drop rolls in batches of three and cook for one minute. **Serves eight to ten.**

DIPPING SAUCE

Don't even think of serving Vegetarian Moon Rolls without this spectacular sauce. You've been warned.

3 cloves garlic, finely minced
1 inch fresh ginger, finely minced
½ cup apricot preserves
½ cup orange marmalade
4 tablespoons rice vinegar (and/or sake)

Use enough liquid to make a smooth, but not runny, consistency.
Serve with Chinese hot mustard and let everyone make their own dipping sauce by blending the two together.

PROSCIUTTO WITH MELON

This is a classic appetizer. It is also great with a loaf of crusty bread or you can wrap the prosciutto around figs. Or spread some goat cheese on sliced prosciutto and wrap around grilled asparagus.

1 melon, cut into six wedges
18 paper-thin prosciutto slices

Place one melon wedge on each of six plates. Arrange three prosciutto slices alongside melon or drape over melon and serve. **Six servings.**

SOUPS

THAI CHICKEN AND COCONUT SOUP

2 tablespoons olive oil
1 red onion, chopped
4 garlic cloves, chopped
2 teaspoons ground cumin
1 small jalapeño, finely chopped
1 lemongrass stock, bruised
Juice of three limes
4 cups chicken stock
2 cups coconut milk
1 pound boneless chicken breast, thinly sliced
Fresh cilantro for garnish

In a large soup pot sauté the onions, garlic, cumin and jalapeno for 10 minutes. Add the stock, lime juice, coconut milk and lemongrass stalk and bring to a boil. Stir in the chicken and simmer uncovered for about 10 minutes until the chicken is tender. Serve at once with a cilantro garnish. **Serves four to six.**

PEAR AND BUTTERNUT SQUASH SOUP

I love butternut squash anything. It's so simple to boil, cut and easily create a myriad of soups. Here the pear takes a simple butternut squash soup recipe and adds a whole new element. The flavor just rolls off your tongue and satisfies like no other squash soup.

(Note for vegetarians: omit the bacon. Sautee veggies in 1 tablespoon olive oil and use soy milk for the heavy cream. Replace chicken stock with vegetable stock).

6 strips bacon, chopped
1 onion, peeled and chopped
4 cups chicken stock
4 cups peeled butternut squash cubes
3 large pears, peeled, cored and cubed
¾ cup chopped celery
1 teaspoon thyme
1 cup heavy cream
Salt and freshly ground pepper to taste
Chopped fresh thyme for garnish

Sauté bacon in a large stockpot until crisp; remove from pan, drain on paper towels and crumble. Remove all but one tablespoon bacon grease from pot; add onion and sauté over medium heat until browned. Add stock, squash, pears and celery to pot. Bring to a boil; reduce heat and simmer, covered, for 30 minutes. Let cool slightly, and then with an immersion blender or in a blender or food processor, puree mixture until smooth. Return back to pot and add thyme and bacon. Simmer for 10 minutes more. Stir in cream and season to taste with salt and pepper. Ladle into bowls and sprinkle with chopped fresh thyme.

AVGOLEMONO (GREEK LEMON SOUP)

A Greek friend made his grandmother's soup recipe for me and I loved it so much I wanted to recreate it in my own kitchen. He was understandably skittish about parting with that family jewel of a recipe, so I tinkered until I came up with the following version, replacing pasta shells with orzo for a lighter soup. Don't tell Peter, but I like mine even better.

4 eggs
1 cup orzo pasta
8 cups chicken stock
2 cups chicken breasts, cooked and chopped
1 cup fresh lemon juice
6 sprigs parsley, chopped
Zest of one lemon
Salt and pepper to taste

Bring the stock to boil in a four-quart soup pot and add the orzo. Cook covered until the orzo is tender, about 15 minutes. Whisk together the eggs and lemon juice. Remove the soup from heat and add the egg mixture. Continue to cook for a moment until all thickens. Remove from the heat again and add chopped parsley, lemon zest, lemon juice and chicken. Serve when it is all heated through. **Serves four to six.**

CREAMY WINTER SQUASH & APPLE SOUP

4 pounds assorted winter squashes (such as Turban, Butternut, Hubbard, Australian Blue)
1 tablespoon ground cumin
1 tablespoon ground coriander
2 teaspoons minced fresh sage, or ¾ teaspoon dried rubbed sage
1 ½ tablespoons ground allspice
3 tablespoons olive oil
1 onion, finely chopped
1 tart apple (such as Granny Smith) cored, peeled and grated
14 ½ ounces of chicken or vegetable broth (best if you make your own from organic chicken or veggies)
1 cup Greek yogurt
Finely chopped pine nuts and sage for garnish, or toasted squash seeds

Preheat oven to 375°. Cut squash in half, scoop out seeds and fibers. Place cut side down on shallow baking pan. Bake for 45 to 75 minutes, or until very soft. Let cool, then scrape the squash meat from the skin. Mash the squash and set aside.

While squash is baking, combine cumin and coriander in a dry sauté pan. Toast, stirring constantly until the spices begin to change color and when it just begins to smoke remove from heat and set aside to cool in small bowl. Add sage and allspice.

Heat olive oil over medium heat in a heavy large saucepan. Add onion, cook until soft but not brown. Stir in the spice mixture. Add the apple. Increase heat and cook uncovered until apple mixture becomes dry and begins to brown. Add the broth and scrape up ingredients up from the bottom of pot. Stir in squash, bring to simmer and cook for 30 minutes. Puree the soup in blender or food processor in several batches. Season with salt and pepper to taste.

Add the yogurt a little at a time. It's easiest to do this by putting some soup in a bowl and whisking a dollop of yogurt in, then pour back into the soup pot, and then repeat until yogurt is gone. Stir soup well. **Serves four to six.**

PUMPKIN AND GRUYERE SOUP

Look for sugar pumpkins for this recipe, the kind you would traditionally use to bake a pie, not a carving pumpkin. It's a more condensed pumpkin flavor, easier to work with and you can still roast the seeds.

One 5-6 pound pumpkin
¼ cup butter
1 onion, finely chopped
6 cups chicken or vegetable stock
2 cups heavy cream
Zest of one orange
Juice of one orange
Juice of one lemon
1 inch fresh ginger, finely chopped
1 pound Gruyere cheese, shredded

Cut pumpkin in half, scoop out strings and seeds. Cut away the hard peel and coarsely chop the flesh. In a large soup pan melt the butter over medium heat. Add the onion and sauté five minutes. Add the stock and pumpkin and bring to a boil. Reduce heat, cover and simmer until pumpkin is tender, about 45 minutes. Blend or process the soup. Return the puree to pot and stir in the cream, orange, lemon and ginger. Reserve a little cheese for garnish (perhaps with some fresh sage). Sprinkle into the soup. Stir over low heat until cheese melts. Serve immediately. **Serves four to six.**

CARROT ORANGE GINGER SOUP

1 tablespoon olive oil
2 medium red onions, sliced
4 inches fresh ginger
6 cups vegetable stock
2 cups orange juice
Zest of one orange
2 pounds carrots cut into 2-inch pieces
Pinch of kosher salt
½ teaspoon white pepper

Heat the olive oil in a large stockpot over low heat and sauté onions until they are translucent. Roughly chop the peeled ginger and add to the onions and sauté together for about three minutes. Increase heat and add the stock and carrots. Simmer over medium heat until the carrots are tender. Add the orange juice and zest and cook for five minutes. Season with salt and pepper. Purée carefully and serve. **Serves four to six**.

SALADS & SIDES

POMEGRANATE, BEETS, FENNEL & BLOOD ORANGE SALAD

The joy of this salad is that beets are widely available pre-cooked. (If possible, avoid using canned beets in this recipe; they tend to be tinny and tart.) The pomegranate seeds and vinegar are also now in most every market, making this elegant offering an interesting, colorful and delicious salad for your next gathering.

8 medium beets
6 tablespoons olive oil
1 teaspoon salt
½ teaspoon ground black pepper
¼ cup water
Juice from two blood oranges
4 tablespoons pomegranate vinegar
1 red onion, thinly sliced
1 fennel bulb, coarsely chopped
4 blood oranges, peeled, cut into ¼ inch-thick slices
1 cup pomegranate seeds

Preheat oven to 400°F. Place beets in roasting pan and toss with 3 tablespoons oil, 1 teaspoon salt and ½ teaspoon pepper. Add ¼ cup water. Cover pan with foil; roast beets until knife easily pierces center, about 50 minutes. Cool. Peel beets and cut into $\frac{1}{3}$ inch-thick wedges.

Whisk orange juice, pomegranate vinegar, and remaining 2 tablespoons oil in large bowl to blend. Season vinaigrette with salt and pepper. Add beets, onion, fennel, orange slices, and pomegranate seeds to vinaigrette in bowl; toss. Season salad with salt and pepper. **Serves four to six**.

MIXED GREENS WITH PEARS, GORGONZOLA AND MAPLE SYRUP VINAIGRETTE

VINAIGRETTE:
2 cloves garlic, finely chopped
2 tablespoons Dijon Mustard
1 tablespoon maple syrup
6 tablespoons balsamic vinegar
1 cup olive oil
Fresh ground pepper

Whisk all ingredients together and set aside.

SALAD:
1 bag spinach
1 bag arugula
1 bag Mache
(or any mixture of harvest greens)
3 ripe Asian pears, cored and sliced
6 ounces Gorgonzola

Toss all lettuces together. Lightly toss with dressing. Arrange lettuces on platter. Place pears prettily on top and sprinkle with Gorgonzola and fresh ground pepper. **Serves four to six.**

CLEMENTINE CAESAR SALAD

The Clementine is a juicier and sweeter fruit, offering a more pronounced orange flavor than other varieties. It's a nice counterpoint to the brininess of the anchovy.

1 teaspoon anchovy paste
2 tablespoons Dijon mustard
3 cloves garlic, finely chopped
1 cup Clementine juice
1 tablespoon zest
¾ cup olive oil
2 heads romaine lettuce leaves, chopped
3 cups pumpkin seeds, toasted
2 cups Clementine sections
12 tablespoons Parmesan cheese, grated

Puree the anchovy paste, Dijon mustard, zest and garlic in a food processor until smooth. Add 1 cup orange juice and olive oil in a fine stream, processing constantly. Toss the romaine lettuce with the dressing in a large salad bowl. Divide among six salad plates. Arrange ½ cup pumpkin seeds and ⅓ cup Clementine sections on each plate. Sprinkle each with Parmesan cheese. **Serves four to six.**

SWEET POTATO SALAD

Only recently have we discovered that sweet potatoes have a diverse and beautiful life well beyond the marshmallow and brown sugar creations enjoyed around the holidays. This recipe is great year round for picnics, barbeques and potlucks and really allows the sweet potato flavor to shine.

DRESSING:
¼ cup canola oil or macadamia nut oil
2 tablespoons maple syrup
2 tablespoons orange juice
2 tablespoons red wine vinegar
Juice of one lemon
2 inches ginger, peeled and minced
½ teaspoon cinnamon
¼ teaspoon nutmeg

Whisk all ingredients to blend in small bowl. Season dressing to taste with salt and pepper.

6 pounds red-skinned sweet potatoes (yams), peeled, cut into ¾ inch cubes
1 cup chopped green onions
1 cup chopped fresh parsley
1 cup Macadamia nuts
½ cup golden raisins
½ cup brown raisins

Steam sweet potatoes in batches until potatoes are just tender, about ten minutes per batch. Transfer sweet potatoes to large bowl. Cool to room temperature. Add green onions, parsley, macadamia nuts, and all raisins. Pour dressing over; toss gently to blend. Season salad to taste with salt and pepper. **Serves four to six.**

CITRUS RICE SALAD

4 cups water
2 cups uncooked brown basmati rice
1 ½ teaspoons salt
½ cup orange juice
½ cup olive oil
¼ cup lemon juice
4 teaspoons grated orange zest
2 teaspoons grated lemon zest
1 inch ginger, peeled and grated
30 cherry tomatoes, halved
7 small Persian cucumbers, diced
1 cup sliced green onions
½ cup chopped fresh mint
16 ounces feta cheese, crumbled

Bring water, rice, and salt to boil in heavy medium saucepan over high heat, stirring occasionally. Reduce heat to low; cover and cook until rice is tender and water is absorbed, about 20 minutes. Uncover saucepan and cook rice over very low heat until dry, about five minutes. Transfer rice to large bowl and cool to room temperature.

Whisk orange juice and olive oil, zests and ginger in small bowl to blend.
Add halved tomatoes, cucumbers, green onions, mint, and feta to rice in large bowl. Add dressing; toss to blend. (Can be made eight hours ahead; cover and refrigerate. Bring to room temperature and toss before serving.) **Serves four to six.**

CORN MAQUE CHOUX (a.k.a. SMOTHERED CORN YA DERN FOOL)

A great side for Thanksgiving or Christmas dinner, or any time you want to be a darn fool. The key elements in this dish are spicy, sweet and rich. So before serving, adjust all three if needed with additional cayenne pepper, sugar and butter. Some make it even richer by adding a well-beaten raw egg and evaporated milk (not sweetened condensed milk.) Others combine this dish with boneless chunks of chicken, and serve over rice as a main dish.

7 cups fresh corn off the cob (18 ears) or frozen corn kernels
2 tablespoons cooking oil
1 onion, chopped very fine
1 green pepper, chopped very fine
Salt and pepper to taste
2 cups pork or chicken stock
1/8 to 1/4 cup sugar (to taste)
1/2 teaspoon thyme
1/2 teaspoon basil or 2 bay leaves (your choice, but not both)
1/2 teaspoon paprika
1/2 teaspoon cayenne pepper
1/4 teaspoon black or white pepper
2 tablespoons cream
3 tomatoes, peeled and chopped
1 tablespoon minced parsley
4 tablespoons butter

Cut corn from cob by cutting down through the kernels, then scraping the pulp. Sauté the onion and pepper in oil over medium-high heat. Add the corn and seasonings. If using fresh corn wait until the bottom forms a crust before stirring. If it is sticking excessively, thin with stock. Add remaining ingredients, including one cup of the stock. Bring to a boil then reduce heat to a very low temperature. Simmer covered, 30-45 minutes, stirring to make the flavors blend. **Serves four to six**.

BUTTERNUT SQUASH IN COCONUT MILK

3 tablespoons butter
1 small onion, finely chopped
4 cloves garlic, minced
1 inch fresh ginger, peeled and minced
2 cups unsweetened coconut milk
½ cup packed brown sugar
½ teaspoon red pepper flakes
2 butternut squash, peeled, seeded and cut into 2 inch pieces
1 cup toasted coconut
Fresh cilantro

Heat butter in saucepan over medium heat. Add onions, garlic and ginger and sauté until tender. Add coconut milk, sugar and pepper flakes and cook until sugar is dissolved. Bring mixture to a boil; add squash. Simmer until fork tender (about 30 minutes), stirring occasionally. Remove squash from the pan and place in a serving bowl. Boil remaining liquid until thick, stirring constantly. Toss with the squash and garnish with toasted coconut and fresh cilantro. **Serves four to six**.

BLACK BEAN & RED PAPAYA SALAD

3 tablespoons fresh lime juice
1 tablespoon minced fresh ginger
1 teaspoon honey
4 tablespoons olive oil
1 teaspoon salt
¼ teaspoon fresh ground pepper
2 cups canned black beans, drained and rinsed
2 medium red papayas, peeled, seeded, and cut into ½ inch cubes
½ small red onion, thinly sliced, crosswise
½ cup loosely packed mint leaves, coarsely chopped

Combine lime juice, ginger and honey in small bowl. Whisk in olive oil and season with salt and pepper. Set vinaigrette aside. Combine black beans, papaya and red onion in a large bowl and toss together. Pour vinaigrette over and toss again. Cover with plastic wrap and refrigerate for 30 minutes. Add mint, toss again, and serve. **Serves four to six**.

POMEGRANATE AND QUINCE CHICKEN SALAD

The quince was used as a love offering to Venus back in the day, and is finding its way to a myriad of recipes today. If you can't locate one at your farmers' market or specialty food store, an apple is a fine substitution.

4 poached or grilled chicken breasts
1 cup pomegranate juice
½ cup rice vinegar
¼ cup lemon juice
¾ cup olive oil
6 cups mixed baby greens
½ cup pomegranate seeds
½ cup poached quince

TO POACH THE QUINCE:
2 medium quinces
2 cups water
¾ cup sugar
½ cup honey
2 teaspoons lemon juice
2 tablespoons vanilla
½ teaspoon cinnamon

Peel, quarter, and core quinces. Cut quarters crosswise into $1/8$ inch-thick slices. In a 3-quart heavy saucepan bring quinces, water, sugar, honey, lemon juice, vanilla and cinnamon to a boil. Reduce heat and simmer mixture, stirring occasionally, 2 ½ hours (quince will be deep pinkish orange). Drain quince in a large sieve and transfer to paper towels. Pat quince dry and cool. Chill quince, covered, at least 1 hour. This could be done the day before.

In a small saucepot reduce pomegranate juice by one half until syrupy. Allow pomegranate juice to cool and place in a stainless steel bowl. Whisk in rice vinegar, lemon juice and slowly add in olive oil. Adjust seasoning. In a bowl mix greens, pomegranate seeds and vanilla poached quince. Toss with a little vinaigrette. Place salad in the center of a large plate. Slice chicken breasts and arrange on top. Drizzle a little vinaigrette around and serve. **Serves four to six.**

CURRIED LOBSTER AND MANGO SALAD

DRESSING:
2 mangoes, cubed
3 tablespoons fresh lime juice
1 inch ginger, minced
2 teaspoons curry powder
3 tablespoons chopped fresh chives
2 tablespoons shallots, minced

SALAD:
1 red bell pepper, thinly sliced
3 celery stalks, chopped
2 mangoes, cubed
½ cup fresh cilantro leaves
White pepper
2 pounds cooked lobster tail meat, chopped

Place mangoes, lime juice, ginger and curry powder in blender. Blend until smooth. Stir in chives and shallots. Season to taste with salt and white pepper.

In a large bowl toss together bell pepper, celery, mangoes and cilantro. Add lobster. Drizzle some dressing over and toss lightly. Season with salt and white pepper to taste. **Serves four to six.**

SHRIMP AND BERRY SALAD WITH CITRUS VINAIGRETTE

1 basket blackberries
1 basket raspberries
¼ cup pine nuts
2 firm-ripe avocados
1 teaspoon fresh lime juice
1 pound large shrimp, shelled and deveined
2 cups each baby spinach and arugula (or your favorite mix of greens)

VINAIGRETTE:
¼ cup fresh orange juice
Juice of one lime
¼ teaspoon ginger, finely chopped
6 tablespoons cilantro, finely chopped
½ tablespoon jalapeño pepper, finely chopped
¾ cup canola oil

Whisk together vinaigrette ingredients with salt and pepper to taste. Set aside.

Quarter avocados lengthwise, then pit and peel. Cut lengthwise into ¼ inch-thick slices. Drizzle with lime juice and season with salt and pepper.

Prepare barbeque or stovetop grill (medium-high heat). Pour ¼ cup dressing into small bowl. Reserve remainder for salad. Brush shrimp with dressing from small bowl and grill until opaque in center, turning occasionally, about five minutes.

In a large serving dish or bowl toss together spinach, arugula, berries and pine nuts and dress lightly. Arrange avocados and shrimp on top of salad and serve. **Serves four to six.**

SPINACH SALAD WITH BAKED GOAT CHEESE, PEARS AND DRIED CHERRIES

Baked goat cheese is a melt in your mouth deliciousness. There's a lot going on in this salad and somehow the flavors and textures come together beautifully. It's one of my most requested salads.

12 cups baby spinach, rinsed and dried
1½ cups dried cherries
2 medium pears, sliced
1 cup pecans, toasted
2 cups panko (Japanese bread crumbs)
1 tablespoon mustard powder
2 eggs
16 ounces goat cheese, sliced into 16 pieces
¼ cup red wine vinegar
4 tablespoons Dijon mustard
1 small shallot, finely chopped
4 cloves garlic, finely chopped
½ cup olive oil plus more for brushing
Salt and pepper to taste

Whisk together vinegar, mustard, shallot, garlic and olive oil. Add salt and pepper and set aside. In a large salad bowl toss together baby spinach, pecans and set aside. In a bowl whisk eggs and mustard together. Place panko on a plate. Place each slice of cheese into egg mixture, then cover thoroughly with panko. Freeze for 30 minutes until firm. Remove from the freezer and brush with olive oil. Bake in a pre-heated 450-degree oven until panko is golden brown and cheese is slightly soft. Toss the salad with dressing and place baked cheese on top and serve. **Serves four to six.**

GRILLED SALMON AND STARFRUIT SALAD

1 ½ pounds salmon fillet, cut into 4 pieces
2 starfruit, cut crosswise into ¼ inch thick slices
8 cups torn mixed baby greens
1 cucumber, peeled, halved lengthwise and thinly sliced
3 green onions, sliced
½ cup balsamic vinegar
3 tablespoons Dijon mustard
3 cloves garlic, minced
1 teaspoon thyme
1 ½ cups olive oil
Salt & pepper to taste

In a small jar mix together balsamic, Dijon, garlic, thyme and oil. Shake well.

Arrange the salmon on a lightly oiled grilling tray or broiler pan. Place one quarter cup of the dressing in a small bowl. Brush some dressing over the fish. Grill or broil, uncovered, for five minutes. Turn the fish and arrange the starfruit alongside it on the grilling tray. Brush the fish and starfruit lightly with the dressing. Return to the grill. Cook for 3 to 6 minutes longer, or until the fish flakes easily with a fork.

Combine the lettuce and cucumber in a large salad bowl. Add the remaining dressing and toss to coat well. Divide the salad evenly among four dinner plates. Place one piece of salmon on the center of each salad. Arrange the star fruit slices around each salad plate. Sprinkle with green onions. **Serves four to six**.

MINT SOBA NOODLES

12 ounces dried soba noodles
⅓ cup rice vinegar
1 tablespoon canola oil
3 tablespoons soy sauce
1 ¼ teaspoons sugar
1 teaspoon red pepper flakes
½ cup chopped fresh mint
1 ½ cups thinly sliced scallions

Cook noodles in a large pot of boiling water until just tender, about 5 minutes, then drain in a colander. Rinse under cold water to stop cooking, and then drain well. While noodles are cooking, stir together vinegar, oil, soy sauce, sugar, red pepper, and salt until sugar is dissolved. Toss noodles with dressing, mint and scallions. Serve at once. **Serves four to six**.

WATERMELON AND MANGO WITH LIMES AND MINT

A hot weather favorite, I first made this for my daughter Emma when she had a summer cold and no appetite. I wanted to prepare something she would eat more than a bite of and also something that would perk her up. These are all of her favorite flavors and now she requests it whenever the fruits are in season.

1 (4 pound) watermelon, cut into 1-inch chunks
2 mangoes (1 ¾ pounds total), peeled, pitted, and cut into 1-inch chunks
1 tablespoon fresh lime juice, or to taste
1 teaspoon finely grated fresh lime zest
½ cup mint leaves

Toss together all ingredients and chill, covered, stirring occasionally, two hours. **Serves six**.

MAINS

ROAST CHICKEN WITH PEAR

The key to this is having a mushy and very ripe pear. The pear juice infuses into the chicken and it's absolutely one of the most brilliant things you've ever tasted. The blend of the rosemary and thyme pulls it all together, delivering a real sweet and earthy flavor.

1 roasting chicken
1 very ripe pear
2 sprigs fresh rosemary
2 sprigs fresh thyme
3 cloves garlic
2 onions
Salt
Pepper
Melted butter for basting

Peel the onions and slice them in thin circles. Separate them slightly and line them in a roasting pan. Rinse the chicken with cold water and pat dry, removing all the neck and liver. Sprinkle the skin with salt and pepper. Place the whole pear, the garlic, rosemary and thyme into the cavity of the chicken. Place the chicken on top of the onions and baste with the melted butter. Roast at 425° for 1 hour and 15 minutes. **Serves two to four.**

CRANBERRY CHICKEN

2 tablespoons olive oil
6 shallots, finely chopped
2 teaspoons thyme
2 teaspoons sage
½ teaspoon white pepper
3 cups chicken stock
1 bag fresh cranberries (12 ounces)
½ cup sugar
1 teaspoon cornstarch
8 chicken breasts

To bake the chicken, I slather with butter, thyme and sage. Bake at 400° for approximately 45 minutes until cooked through and golden.

Sautee shallots over medium heat until tender. Add sage and thyme and sauté for one minute. Add stock and simmer for 10 minutes. Add cranberries and sugar and boil until cranberries burst, about 10 minutes. In a small bowl whisk together the cornstarch with two tablespoons of the sauce. Whisk it in to heated mixture and return to a boil, cook for 5 minutes longer. Add white pepper. Pour a generous amount of sauce over the chicken. **Serves four to six.**

LIME TARRAGON CHICKEN

4 boneless skinless chicken breast halves
¼ cup olive oil
3 tablespoons fresh lime juice
4 teaspoons tarragon, finely chopped

Arrange chicken in single layer in glass casserole or pie plate. Season with salt and pepper. Whisk oil, lime juice and tarragon in small bowl to blend. Pour marinade over chicken and turn to coat. Let stand at room temperature 20 minutes.

Preheat broiler or prepare barbecue (medium-high heat). Transfer chicken to broiler pan or barbecue. Season with salt and pepper. Broil until just cooked through, about 3 minutes per side. **Serves four.**

PECAN PEACH CHICKEN

I was cooking dinner for a date, a Southern boy who told me the best chicken he ever ate was his mama's peach chicken. Not wanting to tinker with family tradition, I set out to create my own peach chicken. Since peaches and pecans are quintessential Southern fare and a perfect combination, I coated the chicken with pecans for crunchiness and used the peach for a sauce to sweeten the deal. It was an amazing dinner that guaranteed me a second date. Peachy keen, indeed!

5 large peaches, peeled and pitted and mashed
1 cup white wine (or chicken stock)
1 teaspoon cinnamon
⅛ cup sugar
6 shakes green Tabasco
½ cup flour
1 egg, beaten
¾ cup pecans, finely minced
2 tablespoons canola oil
2 chicken breasts, boned, skinned, split in half and slightly flattened

In a large skillet, combine the peaches, white wine, cinnamon, sugar and green Tabasco. Stir gently over medium heat until the peaches are tender and heated through. The sauce will reduce slightly and thicken. Set aside and keep warm. Place the flour on a flat plate, the egg in a large bowl and the chopped pecans on a flat plate. In a large skillet, heat the oil until hot. Dip chicken into flour and shake off any excess. Then dip into egg and finally into chopped pecans. Sauté three minutes on each side until cooked. Place on dinner plate and top with peach sauce. **Serves two to four.**

GRILLED KEY LIME CHICKEN WITH BLACK BEAN SAUCE

3 pounds chicken breasts, skinless, boneless
1 cup Key lime juice
1 tablespoon honey
¾ cup water
½ teaspoon fresh ground black pepper
1 bunch cilantro
2 tablespoons olive oil
1 inch ginger, peeled and minced
2 cloves garlic, minced

Combine all ingredients except chicken in blender or food processor. Process until combined well. Pour over chicken. Cover and let marinate in the refrigerator overnight. Grill over hot coals, turning once, until done. Garnish with cilantro and lime slices.

BLACK BEAN BAUCE:
1 (15 ounce) can black beans, drained, rinsed
1 quart chicken stock
4 cloves garlic, minced
One bunch of cilantro, chopped
Salt and freshly ground pepper to taste
Pinch cayenne pepper

Prepare sauce while chicken is marinating. Place beans in a large saucepan or soup pan, and add all remaining ingredients. Bring to a boil, and then reduce the heat and simmer, uncovered, for about 1 ½ hours. **Serves four to six.**

APRICOT AND MAYTAG BLUE CHEESE STUFFED CHICKEN

½ cup dried apricots, chopped
2 tablespoons parsley, chopped
4 cloves garlic, minced
½ cup Maytag blue cheese, crumbled
4 chicken breasts

Preheat oven to 375°. Mix apricots, parsley, garlic and cheese in a small bowl. Loosen the skin of chicken breasts and stuff cheese mixture underneath. Press the skin down. Place breasts in a greased baking dish. Bake about 40 minutes or until done. **Serves four to six**.

BLOOD ORANGE BARBECUED CHICKEN

1 red onion, finely chopped
2 cloves garlic, finely chopped
3 tablespoons butter
⅓ cup honey
3 tablespoons soy sauce
1 teaspoon Asian Chili garlic sauce
(you can substitute Tabasco, to taste)

Juice of one lemon
Juice of two blood oranges
2 tablespoons Blood Orange zest
1 ½ tablespoons cornstarch
3 pounds boneless chicken breasts
3 pounds drumsticks
Olive oil for brushing

To make the sauce, in a small saucepan sauté the onion and garlic in the butter until tender. Add the honey, lemon juice, soy sauce, chili sauce and blood orange zest. Gradually blend the orange juice into the cornstarch; add to the onion mixture. Cook over medium heat, stirring, until thickened. Season chicken with salt and pepper. Lightly brush the chicken drumsticks with oil. Barbecue on a grill six inches above the glowing coals for 20 minutes. Turn and cook 20 minutes longer. Brush the chicken with oil and add to the grill cooking 10 minutes on each side. Brush with sauce. Continue cooking until the chicken is tender, turning and brushing occasionally with sauce. **Serves six**.

FIG AND ORANGE CHICKEN

1 red onion, coarsely chopped
½ cup currants
10 Black Mission Figs or 8 of the larger amber-colored Calimyrna figs, cut into halves
1 ½ cups orange juice
4 teaspoons Worcestershire sauce
1 tablespoon curry powder
1 tablespoon soy sauce
4 cloves garlic, finely chopped
3 pounds chicken pieces or 6 boneless breasts
10 new potatoes, quartered
4 carrots, sliced
Salt and pepper to taste

Place washed chicken, carrots and potatoes in Pyrex or roasting pan. In a medium bowl mix the rest of the ingredients. Pour over chicken and bake at 400° for 35-40 minutes, basting at least twice during cooking. **Serves four.**

TURKEY BURGER WITH CRANBERRIES AND GINGER

When turkey burgers are seasoned like hamburgers, adding cheese and other traditional accompaniments, it just doesn't work for me. You wouldn't pile on cheese and ketchup on your Thanksgiving bird, right? I pulled the components from a traditional turkey dinner and added a little ginger for heat. I prepare them regular sized as well as minis for parties, and they are always a big hit.

1 pound ground turkey
2 scallions, thinly chopped
½ cup dried cranberries, finely chopped
3 cloves garlic, finely chopped
1 inch ginger, finely chopped
¼ teaspoon crushed red pepper
Chinese style mustard
Dijon mustard
Wasabi paste
Splash soy sauce
4 burger buns or rolls
1 cup Asian lettuce mix

In a medium bowl mix the turkey, scallions, cranberries, garlic, ginger, red pepper and soy sauce. Divide into four patties. Over medium coals place on grill (or skillet or stovetop grill) and cook for 10 minutes and flip and cook 5-10 minutes longer. Serve on a bun with ¼ cup Asian lettuce, Chinese style mustard and wasabi mustard. (In a small bowl whisk together ¼ cup Dijon mustard and 1 tablespoon wasabi paste.) **Serves four.**

ORANGE AND VEGETABLE KABOB

1 large sweet onion
1 large orange, unpeeled
1 medium sweet red pepper, cut into 1-inch pieces
1 medium yellow pepper, cut into 1-inch pieces
8 medium fresh mushrooms
8 cherry tomatoes
2 small yellow summer squash, cut into 1-inch slices

MARINADE:
½ cup olive oil or vegetable oil
Juice and zest from one large lemon
Juice and zest from one small orange
3 cloves garlic
1 inch ginger, peeled and minced
1 teaspoon salt
¼ teaspoon pepper

Cut the onion and orange into eight wedges; half each wedge. Alternately thread vegetables and orange pieces onto eight metal or soaked wooden skewers. Place in a shallow oblong dish. In a bowl, whisk together the oil, lemon, ½ the orange and zest, garlic, ginger, salt and pepper. Pour over skewers. Marinate for 15 minutes, turning and basting frequently.

Grill, covered, over indirect heat for 10-15 minutes or until the vegetables are crisp-tender. Brush with orange juice just before serving. **Serves four.**

GRILLED SHRIMP AND GINGER LIME MARINADE

2 pounds shrimp, frozen raw peeled and deveined
1 cup olive or vegetable oil
¼ cup sesame oil
2 tablespoons minced garlic
2 inches ginger, peeled and thinly sliced
½ cup soy sauce
½ teaspoon red pepper
1 lime

In a large bowl combine oils, soy sauce, garlic, ginger, pepper and lime. Drop in the shrimp and stir gently to coat well with the marinade. Let stand at room temperature for one hour. Prepare the grill. Reserving the marinade, arrange the shrimp in one layer in a large grilling basket; close the basket. (You can also skewer them on 8 to 10 inch skewers. Remember if using wood…soak.) Grill the shrimp 3 minutes five inches from heat then brush with marinade and grill for 2 more minutes. Turn and marinade and grill for 3 minutes until the shrimp are cooked through and still moist and firm to the touch. As I have said before with shrimp…don't overcook.

Serve over rice with grilled veggies brushed with the reserve marinade. **Serves four.**

ROASTED SALMON WITH POMEGRANATE AND AVOCADO SALSA

2 teaspoons ground coriander
2 teaspoons sugar
Salt, as needed
1 pomegranate, seeded
½ cup thinly sliced green onion
3 tablespoons fresh lime juice
2 teaspoons finely chopped jalapeño pepper or to taste
1 large clove garlic, chopped finely
2 avocados, preferably Hass, cut in ½-inch dice
1 head hearts of romaine, about 7 ounces
4 center-cut salmon filets the same thickness, 6 to 7 ounces each
1 lime, cut in eighths for garnish

Mix coriander, sugar and 1 teaspoon salt; reserve. Up to 4 hours before serving mix pomegranate seeds, onion, lime juice, jalapeño, and garlic; gently fold in avocado. If holding more than 30 minutes, put plastic wrap against the surface of the salsa, then tightly cover; store in the refrigerator. Remove about 30 minutes before serving. Separate the romaine leaves; wash, then dry thoroughly. Reserve four of the most attractive leaves for garnish. Slice the remaining leaves crosswise in thin shreds; reserve.

To prepare the salmon, rub a generous teaspoon of the reserved seasoning mixture over each piece. Arrange the salmon on a baking sheet, skin-side down. Roast at 500 about 11 minutes for medium rare (salmon should be spongy when pressed with a finger at its thickest part) and 13 minutes for medium-well (salmon should be just firm when pressed with a finger at its thickest part).

While the salmon cooks, mound ¼ of the shredded romaine on each of four serving plates. Top with ½ cup salsa. When salmon is done, let it cool slightly-- it should be warm but not hot. Place a piece of salmon on each plate; garnish each with a reserved romaine leaf and two lime wedges. **Serves four.**

CHILEAN SEA BASS WITH CRANBERRY BUTTER SAUCE

3 tablespoons orange juice
1 cup cranberries
1 teaspoon pumpkin pie spice
1 cup vegetable stock
4 (8 ounce) Chilean sea bass fillets
¼ cup all-purpose flour
½ cup butter
⅓ cup shallots, minced

In a one-quart pan, combine orange juice, cranberries, pumpkin pie spice and stock. Bring to boiling over high heat. Cover pan, remove from heat and set aside.

Rinse sea bass and pat dry. Lightly dust with flour. In a 12-inch frying pan over medium-high heat, melt 1 ½ tablespoons butter. Add the fish; cook until fish is opaque in thickest part about 3 minutes on each side. Place on serving dish; keep warm. Add 1 tablespoon of butter and the shallots to pan; stir over medium heat until shallots are soft. Add cranberry mixture and boil, uncovered, until reduced to ¾ cup. Reduce heat. Add remaining butter in one piece and stir constantly to incorporate it into sauce. Pour sauce over fish; serve at once. **Serves four.**

MAHI MAHI WITH BLOOD ORANGE SALSA

4 blood oranges
2 avocados, chopped
1 red onion, chopped
3 cloves garlic
1 inch ginger, minced
1 small jalapeño, minced
Juice of 2-3 limes (to coat)
2 teaspoons olive oil
4 6-ounce mahi mahi fillets

Using small sharp knife, cut peel and white pith from orange. Working over small bowl, cut between membranes to release segments. Add avocado, onion, garlic, ginger, jalapeño, and lime juice to oranges in bowl; stir gently to blend. Season salsa to taste with salt.

Heat oil in heavy medium skillet over medium-high heat. Sprinkle fish with salt and pepper. Add fish to skillet and sauté until brown and cooked through, about 5 minutes per side.

Place one fillet on each of four plates. Generously spoon salsa on top of fish to serve. **Serves four.**

SWORDFISH WITH RED GRAPEFRUIT

2 Texas Red grapefruits
2 tablespoons white wine
¼ cup vegetable oil
1 garlic clove, minced
¾ teaspoon ground cumin
½ teaspoon chili powder
¼ teaspoon salt
2 small jalapeño peppers
4 swordfish steaks, 6 ounces each
1 teaspoon butter
2 tablespoons chopped cilantro

Juice one grapefruit; measure ½ cup juice. Reserve other grapefruit for sections. In a medium bowl, combine juice, wine, oil, garlic, spices and salt; mix well. Set aside three tablespoons of marinade for basting during grilling of swordfish. Cut jalapenos into ½ inch pieces; add to remaining marinade. Place swordfish in a shallow dish. Pour marinade over swordfish. Cover and refrigerate at least one hour. Heat the grill or coals. Peel and section remaining grapefruit; set aside. Drain marinade from dish into a saucepan. Stir in cornstarch and butter, stirring well. Bring mixture to a boil and cook over medium heat two more minutes until thickened. Remove peppers. Stir in cilantro. Keep sauce warm. Grill swordfish about 10 minutes per inch of thickness or until done, basting occasionally. To serve, place swordfish on a platter or serving plates, spoon a few tablespoons sauce on swordfish and garnish with a few grapefruit sections. **Serves four.**

GINGER SOY SALMON

When Emma was three years old her favorite food was "pink chicken." Who knew she was creating a sweet and savory food trend with this zesty and simple salmon dish?

4- 6 ounce salmon fillets
Juice and zest of 5 tangerines or 3 oranges
¼ cup brown sugar
¼ cup soy sauce
1-inch ginger, peeled and finely chopped
¼ to ½ teaspoon crushed red pepper

In a bowl mix all but the salmon. I like to marinade the fish in the sauce for about one hour. Grill over high heat for about seven minutes per side. **Serves four.**

GRILLED CHILEAN SEA BASS WITH WATERMELON SALSA

2 cucumbers, finely chopped
2 cups finely chopped red watermelon
1 red onion, finely chopped
1 seeded jalapeno chili, minced
2 cloves garlic, minced
1 inch ginger, minced
¼ cup chopped fresh cilantro
1 teaspoon fresh lime juice
¾ teaspoon salt
6 (six ounce) pieces Chilean sea bass
1 ½ tablespoons olive oil

Prepare gas or charcoal grill for cooking. If using charcoal, open vents on bottom of grill, then light charcoal. Charcoal fire is medium-hot when you can hold your hand five inches above rack for three to four seconds. If using a gas grill, preheat burners on high, covered, 10 minutes, then reduce heat to moderately high.

Toss together cucumber, watermelon, onion, chili, cilantro, lime juice, garlic, ginger and salt. (Do not make salsa more than 1 hour ahead or it will become watery.)

Pat fish dry, then brush with oil and season with salt. Grill fish, on lightly oiled grill rack, turning over once, until just cooked through, 8 to 9 minutes total. Serve fish topped with salsa. **Serves six.**

CAJUN SALMON WITH CHIPOTLE SQUASH AND MANGO SALSA

1 large butternut squash
1 small can of chipotles
2 tablespoons butter, unsalted
¼ teaspoon chili powder
¼ teaspoon salt
¼ cup cream
Pinch salt

4 (6 ounce) fillets of salmon
2 tablespoons butter, melted
1 teaspoon cayenne
1 teaspoon ground cumin
1 teaspoon dried thyme
2 teaspoons paprika
Salt and pepper to taste

Preheat oven to 350° degrees.
Cut the butternut squash in half lengthwise and scoop out the seeds. Brush the cut sides with a little olive oil and place cut side down on a cookie sheet lined with aluminum foil. Roast squash in oven until easily pierced with a fork. (About 30 minutes.) Scoop out the cooked squash into a food processor. Add two chipotle peppers, two tablespoons of butter, chili powder, salt, and cream. Puree until a smooth consistency. Meanwhile rinse off each portion of salmon and pat dry. Mix all the spices together in a bowl. Brush both sides of each fillet with butter. Sprinkle a little Cajun spice onto each side and lightly press the spices against the fish. Heat a heavy skillet until it is smoking hot. Place the fillets in the skillet. Cook for 1 - 2 minutes and turn the fillets over. Cook until the salmon is firm and cooked through (about 5 minutes).

Spread a portion of the chipotle squash puree onto each plate. Place the salmon fillet on top of squash and top with mango salsa. **Serves four.**

MANGO SALSA:

2 mangoes
Juice of 2-3 limes
Juice of 1 lemon
¼ cup very finely slivered fresh ginger
1 red onion, cut into thin slivers

1 red pepper, thinly sliced
1 to 2 small jalapeño, minced
½ cup coarsely cut cilantro
Pinch salt, to pop the flavors

Mix lime and lemon juices, salt, ginger and onion. Add jalapeño. Toss together mangoes, onions and red pepper. Mix with lime mixture Just before serving, stir in cilantro. Best served within an hour or two of mixing.

BRISKET WITH PORTOBELLO AND DRIED CRANBERRIES

1 cup red wine
1 cup beef stock
½ cup frozen cranberry juice cocktail concentrate, thawed
¼ cup all purpose flour
1 large onion, sliced
6 garlic cloves, chopped
1 sprig rosemary, chopped
1 sprig thyme, chopped
1 (4 pound) trimmed flat-cut brisket
12 ounces medium Portobello mushrooms, thinly sliced
1 cup dried cranberries

Preheat oven to 300°. Whisk wine, stock, cranberry concentrate and flour to blend in medium bowl; pour into 15 x 10 x 2-inch roasting pan. Mix in onion, garlic, thyme and rosemary. Sprinkle brisket on all sides with salt and pepper. Place brisket, fat side up, in roasting pan. Spoon some of wine mixture over. Cover pan tightly with heavy-duty foil.

Bake brisket until very tender, basting with pan juices every hour, about 3 ½ hours. Transfer brisket to plate; cool 1 hour at room temperature. Thinly slice brisket across grain. Arrange slices in pan with sauce, overlapping slices slightly. Preheat oven to 350°F. Place mushrooms and cranberries in sauce around brisket. Cover pan with foil. Bake until mushrooms are tender and brisket is heated through, about 30 minutes. Transfer sliced brisket and sauce to platter and serve. **Serves six.**

GRILLED LAMB CHOPS WITH A SPICY MANGO SAUCE

2 mangoes
2 shallots
½ cup lime juice
⅛ teaspoon cayenne (to taste)
4 (½ inch thick) center-cut shoulder lamb chops (about ¾ pound each)
Fresh cilantro, chopped
1 lime, squeezed

Prepare grill. Peel, pit, and coarsely chop mango. Finely chop shallots. In a blender purée mango and shallot with lime juice, cayenne, and salt and pepper to taste until smooth. Transfer sauce to a bowl and if too thick whisk in some water, 1 tablespoon at a time. Pat lamb dry and season with salt and pepper. Grill lamb on a lightly oiled rack set 5 to 6 inches over glowing coals about 4 minutes on each side for medium-rare. Sprinkle with cilantro and serve with lime wedges. **Serves four.**

PASTA & BREADS

PUMPKIN RISOTTO

3 tablespoons butter
1 tablespoon olive oil
1 onion, diced
4 cloves garlic, minced
1 ½ cups Arborio rice
1 cup diced pumpkin
3 to 4 cups hot vegetable stock
½ cup Parmesan cheese, grated
Salt and pepper to taste
Fresh sage for garnish

Heat butter and oil together in a large saucepan. Sautee the onion and garlic. Add the rice and cook, stirring until the rice is coated in the oil mix about 1 minute. Stir in the pumpkin. Pour over 1 cup of the hot stock.

Cook, stirring often until the liquid is almost all absorbed. You don't want the liquid to be boiling in with the rice, just a gentle simmer. Continue stirring and adding stock one cup at a time until the stock is all absorbed and the rice is tender, about 20 minutes. Stir in the Parmesan cheese. Serve immediately. **Serves four.**

FETTUCCINE WITH FIGS AND PANCETTA

I love the sweet and savory flavors in this unusual pasta dish. The figs offer the sweet, the pancetta offers the savory and the rosemary gives it a beautiful finish.

1 cup pancetta, finely chopped
1 small red onion, finely chopped
4 garlic cloves, finely chopped
1 sprig rosemary, finely chopped
2 tablespoons olive oil
½ cup dry white wine
1 cup chicken stock
¾ pound firm-ripe fresh figs, trimmed and quartered lengthwise
2 tablespoons parsley, finely chopped
Juice of one lemon
1 pound fettuccine
Fresh Parmesan

Heat oil in large sauté pan. Add pancetta and sauté for 2 minutes. Add the onion, garlic and rosemary and sauté for 5 minutes longer. Stir in wine and bring to a boil, stirring occasionally. Remove from heat and stir in stock, figs, parsley, half of pancetta and lemon juice.

Cook fettuccine in a large pot of boiling salted water until al dente. Reserve ½ cup cooking water, and then drain pasta in a colander.

Add fettuccine to fig mixture with ¼ cup reserved cooking water and salt and pepper to taste. Heat over low heat, tossing gently and adding more cooking water if mixture becomes dry, until just heated through.

Serve pasta with the remaining pancetta and freshly shaved Parmesan on top. **Serves four to six.**

LEMON CREAM FETTUCCINE

1 pound asparagus
2 large shallots
3 lemons
1 pound dried fettuccine
4 tablespoons butter
1 ½ cups heavy cream

Trim asparagus and diagonally cut into ¼-inch-thick slices. Finely chop shallots. Finely grate enough lemon zest to measure 1 ½ teaspoons and squeeze enough juice to measure 3 tablespoons.

Fill 6-quart pasta pot three fourths full with salted water and bring to a boil for asparagus and pasta. Have ready a bowl of ice and cold water. Cook asparagus in boiling water until crisp-tender, about 3 minutes, and with a slotted spoon transfer to ice water to stop cooking. Reserve water in pot over low heat, covered. Drain asparagus.

In a deep 12-inch heavy skillet cook shallots in butter with salt and pepper to taste over moderately low heat, stirring, until softened, about 5 minutes. Stir in cream and zest and simmer, stirring occasionally, until slightly thickened, about 10 minutes. Stir in 2 tablespoons lemon juice and remove skillet from heat. Return water in pot to a boil. Cook pasta in boiling water, stirring occasionally, until al dente. Drain pasta in a colander and add to sauce with asparagus, remaining tablespoon lemon juice, and salt and pepper to taste. Heat mixture over low heat, gently tossing until just heated through. **Serves four to six.**

LEMON ROSEMARY RISOTTO

4 tablespoons unsalted butter
1 tablespoon olive oil
1 medium yellow onion, finely chopped
2 cups Arborio rice
6 cups chicken stock
3 teaspoons finely grated lemon zest
⅔ cup finely grated Parmesan cheese
2 sprigs fresh rosemary, finely chopped
Salt and pepper to taste

In a large saucepan or sauté pan, heat 2 tablespoons of butter and 1 tablespoon olive oil over medium heat. When the butter foams, add the onion and cook for 5 to 7 minutes on medium heat until the onion is pale, soft and translucent. Place the stock in a separate saucepan and place over medium heat to warm it through. Once it has become hot, reduce the heat to keep the temperature but not to boil the stock. You simply want to keep it hot so that when you add it to the rice, the temperature doesn't drop. Add the rice and lemon rind to the onion mixture. Stir to combine and to coat all the grains in the hot butter and oil. Begin to add the hot stock, adding about 1 cup at a time and stirring continuously until each cup of stock is absorbed before adding the next. Continue to add the stock, a cup at a time, and continue to stir, until the rice is al dente. This will take about 20 minutes. Depending on your rice, you may not need all 6 cups of stock so start tasting your rice after you've added 5 cups. When the rice is al dente, remove from the heat and add the Parmesan and remaining 2 tablespoons of butter. Stir to combine. Sprinkle with rosemary and season with salt and freshly ground pepper. Serve immediately. **Serves four.**

ROASTED GARLIC, CRANBERRY AND ROSEMARY BISCUITS

2 ¼ cups all-purpose flour
2 teaspoons baking powder
½ teaspoon baking soda
1 teaspoon salt
1 ½ sticks unsalted butter—10 tablespoons cut into ½ inch cubes and chilled, 2 tablespoons melted
3 cloves garlic, minced and sautéed
1 sprig rosemary, chopped
½ cup chopped dried cranberries
½ cup chopped toasted walnuts
1 cup buttermilk, chilled

Preheat the oven to 425°. In a large bowl, whisk the flour, baking powder, baking soda and salt. Add the chilled butter and use a pastry blender or two knives to cut the butter into the flour until it is the size of peas. Stir in garlic, rosemary, cranberries and walnuts. Stir in the buttermilk just until the dough is moistened.

Lightly dust a work surface with flour. Turn the dough out onto the surface and knead just until it comes together. Pat the dough into a ½-inch-thick disk. Using a floured 2 ¼-inch round cookie cutter, stamp out biscuit rounds as closely together as possible. Gather the scraps and knead them together 2 or 3 times, then flatten the dough and stamp out more biscuit rounds. Pat the remaining scraps together and gently press them into a biscuit. Transfer the biscuits to a large baking sheet and brush the tops with melted butter. Bake the biscuits for 20 minutes, or until golden. **Serves eight.**

JALAPEÑO CORNBREAD

I like to serve this with a vegetarian chili or at parties as part of a buffet. If it's a larger event, I make several types of cornbread and this one *always* goes first.

4 eggs
1 cup buttermilk
2 cups corn, fresh, frozen or canned
2 sticks melted butter
4 jalapeño peppers, finely chopped
2 cups cornmeal, blue, yellow or white
1 cup shredded sharp Cheddar cheese

Mix in a large bowl. Spray a loaf pan with Bakers Joy. Bake at 350° for about one hour or until golden on top. **Serves eight.**

CRANBERRY-CHIPOTLE COMPOTE

(Makes about 1 quart)

1 tablespoon olive oil
3 medium Fuji apples
3 medium D'Anjou pears
(both peeled and cut into ¼ inch pieces)
¼ cup dried cranberries
¼ cup Grand Marnier
1 pound fresh cranberries
4 ounces chipotle peppers (canned in adobo), chopped fine

3 tablespoons ground cinnamon
½ cup sugar
½ cup dark brown sugar
Zest from one orange
½ cup fresh orange juice
1 teaspoon nutmeg

Heat oil in medium skillet over medium-high heat. Sauté pears, apples & dried cranberries until soft, 3-5 minutes. Add Grand Marnier and deglaze pan. Add fresh cranberries, chipolatas, cinnamon, sugars, zest and orange juice. Stir and simmer for 40-45 minutes until it begins to thicken. Add nutmeg and Grand Marnier; mix well. Refrigerate for 24 hours.

DESSERTS

GREEN TEA AND CHOCOLATE TRUFFLES

Around mid-day I typically enjoy a cup of green tea. One afternoon I was enjoying a piece of chocolate and I was inspired to see how the two would be together. Pretty amazing, actually. The subtle essence and healing power of green tea makes these really special.

2/3 cup heavy cream
2 tablespoons unsalted butter, cut into 4 pieces and softened
2 teaspoons loose green tea leaves
8 ounces semi-sweet chocolate chips
1 cup cocoa powder

In a medium saucepan bring cream and butter to a boil and stir in tea leaves. Remove from heat and let steep 5 minutes. Meanwhile, finely grind chocolate in a food processor and transfer to a bowl.

Pour cream through a fine-mesh sieve onto chocolate, pressing on and discarding tea leaves, then whisk until smooth. Chill mixture covered, until firm, overnight. Drop mixture by rounded teaspoons onto prepared baking sheet. Refrigerate until firm, about three hours.

Place cocoa powder in a bowl. Roll truffles in mixture. Cover with plastic; chill until ready to serve. **Makes two dozen.**

PEAR TART WITH MAYTAG BLUE CHEESE CRUST

2 cups red wine	1 orange, halved	3 cinnamon sticks
1 cup sugar	1 lemon, halved	5 whole cloves
1 cup water	1 inch ginger, peeled	4 pears, peeled and cored

In a large soup pot, place all ingredients except pears and cook over medium heat, stirring occasionally until the sugar is dissolved. Bring to a boil. Reduce heat to simmer and add pears. Poach until tender about 20 minutes. Remove from stove and cool completely. Refrigerate overnight.

PASTRY CREAM:

⅓ cup sugar	3 egg yolks
1 cup milk	¼ cup butter
2 ½ tablespoons cornstarch	2 teaspoons vanilla

In a medium saucepan mix half the sugar to the milk and bring to a boil, stirring constantly. In a medium bowl whisk together the rest of the sugar and cornstarch and yolks. Once the milk is boiling pour ¼ of the milk mixture into the egg mixture, whisking constantly. Pour the egg mixture into the rest of the milk mixture and return to the heat whisking until the cream thickens and comes to a complete boil. Remove from the heat and add the butter and vanilla, whisking until the butter completely melts. Pour into a bowl and cover with plastic until it comes to room temperature.

CRUST:

¾ cups all flour	½ cup crumbled Maytag Blue Cheese
¼ teaspoon salt	Up to 4 tablespoons ice water
5 tablespoons butter	¼ cup raspberry jelly, melted

Cut the butter into tiny pieces (I use a grater) and place in the freezer for 15 minutes. In a medium mixing bowl whisk together the flour and salt. Using a pastry blender cut the butter into the flour until the pieces are the size of rice. Add cheese. Sprinkle 1 tablespoon water over part of the flour mixture and stir very gently with a fork. Push moistened dough to the side of the bowl. Repeat, using 1 tablespoon of water at a time until all the dough is moistened. Roll dough into a ball wrap in plastic and place in the refrigerator for 15 minutes. Roll out to be 10 inches round. Place in a 9-inch tart pan sprayed with Baker's Joy. Bake in a preheated 350° oven until golden about 15 minutes. When cool spread the vanilla cream over the crust. Slice the pears and place them decoratively over the cream. Brush with raspberry jelly and refrigerate for three hours before serving. **Serves six to eight.**

PECAN SWEET POTATO PIE

1 pastry-lined pie shell
2 cups cooked and peeled sweet potatoes
4 ounces butter
½ cup heavy cream
½ cup light brown sugar, packed
2 large eggs, slightly beaten
1 teaspoon vanilla extract
1 teaspoon ground cinnamon
1 teaspoon ground ginger
½ teaspoon ground nutmeg
Pinch salt
2 tablespoons brandy, bourbon, or orange juice
½ cup dark corn syrup
1 cup pecan halves

Prick bottom of piecrust with a fork; bake in preheated 425° oven for 12 minutes. Set aside. Mash sweet potatoes with half of the butter (¼ cup). Let cool. Add heavy cream, brown sugar, eggs, vanilla, spices, and brandy, bourbon or orange juice. Beat until fluffy; turn into piecrust. Bake at 375° for 20 minutes.

Combine remaining ¼ cup butter with corn syrup and pecans; sprinkle evenly over top of pie. Return pie to oven and bake 25 minutes longer, or until a toothpick inserted in center comes out clean. Serve with whipped cream or ice cream. **Serves six to eight.**

MIXED BERRY WITH LAVENDER SHORT CAKE

Lavender grows freely in my garden and I enjoy introducing this aromatic herb to both entrees and desserts to enhance already robust flavors. At the height of berry season, it's a match made in heaven. For parties I make bite-sized portions of the short cake and serve mixed berries and whipped cream in separate bowls so guests can build their own sweet creations.

2 cups flour
1 tablespoon baking powder
3 tablespoons sugar
½ teaspoon salt
3 tablespoons lavender sprigs, finely chopped
½ stick butter, cut into tiny pieces
¾ cup heavy cream
1 quart fresh berries
¼ cup sugar
Splash orange juice
Fresh whipped cream

Spray a cookie sheet with Baker's Joy. Preheat oven to 450°. In a bowl whisk together flour, baking powder salt and sugar. Add the lavender. Cut in the butter until the mixture resembles coarse meal. Lightly stir in cream until the dough is just blended. Drop twelve 3-inch (or smaller if doing minis) rounds of batter from a spoon. Bake for about 12 minutes until golden. Meanwhile, in a large bowl gently mix berries, sugar and orange juice. When ready to serve whip the cream. Split biscuits in half lengthwise. Cover with berries and fresh cream. Serve immediately. **Serves six.**

MEXICAN CHOCOLATE SOUFFLÉ WITH COFFEE SAUCE

2 tablespoons butter
2 tablespoons cornstarch
½ cup heavy cream
1 cup semisweet chocolate chips
3 egg yolks
6 egg whites
1 tablespoon strong coffee
1 teaspoon cinnamon
Pinch of salt
⅓ cup sugar

Preheat oven to 350°. Spray a 1 ½ quart soufflé dish with Baker's Joy. In a saucepan melt the butter and then whisk in the cornstarch and cook for about 2 minutes. Whisk in the cream and continue to stir for 2 minutes. Remove from heat and stir in the chocolate chips and stir until melted. Whisk in the egg yolks, coffee and cinnamon until smooth. Pour into a large bowl. Beat the egg whites with an electric mixture until frothy. Add the salt and continue beating until soft peaks form. Add the sugar and continue beating until they form stiff, shiny peaks. Fold eggs into the chocolate mixture. Gently scrape batter into soufflé dish. Place on a baking sheet and bake for about 35 minutes. Dust with confectioners sugar and serve with sauce on the side.

COFFEE SAUCE:
1 pint vanilla ice cream
3 tablespoons coffee liqueur

Let the ice cream soften for 20 minutes. Place in a bowl and mix in liqueur and stir until blended. Transfer to a bowl and serve. **Serves four.**

24-KARAT CAKE

I happened upon a school's fund-raising cookbook at a garage sale, bought it because I loved some of the home grown recipes and months later when a girlfriend was sifting through my collection she came across the book tucked away on a shelf. Turns out it was the school she attended and the recipe for 24-karat cake was her mother's. I modified the cake a bit, adding more carrots and pineapple and hit it a little harder with cinnamon. I also used less oil and added pumpkin pie spice.

2 cups sifted flour
1 teaspoon salt
2 teaspoons baking powder
1 ½ teaspoons baking soda
2 cups sugar
2 teaspoons cinnamon
2 teaspoons pumpkin pie spice
4 eggs
1 ½ cups cooking oil
2 cups grated carrot
8 ½ ounces crushed pineapple, drained
1 ½ cup chopped nuts

To flour add salt, baking soda, sugar and cinnamon. Mix. Add eggs and cooking oil and mix well. Add carrot, pineapple and nuts. Put in 9x13 greased and floured pan. Bake at 350° for 25 minutes. **Serves eight.**

FROSTING:
½ cup butter
8 ounces cream cheese
2 teaspoons vanilla
1 pound powder sugar

Beat above ingredients until smooth.

LEMON ROSEMARY POUND CAKE

1 cup butter
2 teaspoons rosemary, finely chopped
3 teaspoons lemon zest
4 eggs
1 cup sugar
1 teaspoon vanilla
¼ cup lemon juice
1 teaspoon baking powder
¼ teaspoon salt
2 cups flour

Preheat oven to 350°. Spray a loaf pan with Baker's Joy. In the bowl of an electric mixer beat butter, zest, rosemary and sugar until light and fluffy. Beat in eggs one at a time, then add vanilla. On low speed add flour, baking powder and salt until just blended. Pour into prepared pan and bake for 40 minutes until a wooden pick comes out clean. Cool on wire rack for 15 minutes then remove from pan and cool completely. **Serves eight to twelve.**

CHOCOLATE BEET BUNDT CAKE

Who would have thought? Always looking for things to mix with the perfect food – chocolate – it seemed to me that beets would release their natural sugars and enhance with depth of flavor and color. The color is stunning, the flavor is decadent and most are hard pressed to believe they just reveled in a slice of beet cake.

2 cups all-purpose flour
4 tablespoons unsweetened cocoa powder
1 teaspoon cinnamon
2 teaspoons baking soda
1 tablespoon kosher salt
¾ cup + ¼ cup butter, softened and divided
1 ½ cups packed dark brown sugar

3 eggs, at room temperature
6 ounces 60-70% chocolate, chopped
2 cups beet puree (about 6-7 small-medium beets roasted, peeled, and processed until smooth)
1 tablespoon vanilla
1 tablespoon instant espresso powder

FOR THE GANACHE:
8 ounces 60-70% chocolate, chopped
2 tablespoons unsalted butter, softened
½ cup heavy cream

Preheat the oven to 375°. Spray Bundt pan with Baker's Joy. In a large bowl, combine the flour, cocoa powder, cinnamon, baking soda, salt and sift until evenly distributed. Set aside. Cream ¾ cup butter and the sugar in the base of a standing mixer until light and fluffy. Add the eggs in one at a time and let beat for 3-4 minutes until doubled in volume. While the egg mixture beats, combine the chocolate with the remaining butter and microwave 20 seconds at a time, stirring each time, until melted. Stir until smooth and set aside. Add the vanilla extract to the eggs, followed by the espresso, chocolate and the beet puree and mix until well combined. Add the flour mixture to the beet mixture and mix just until completely and evenly combined. Pour the batter into the prepared Bundt pan with the batter angled so that it is an inch higher on the sides than in the center, and bake at 375° for about 50 minutes or until a tester inserted near the center comes out clean. Cool in the pan for 15 minutes before inverting on a wire rack.

While the cake is cooling, make the ganache by combining the chocolate and butter in a medium bowl. Heat the cream through gently just until it starts to bubble and pour over the chocolate. Stir slowly until the chocolate melts and the ganache becomes smooth and glossy. Pour the ganache over the cooled cake and let set 15-20 minutes before serving. **Serves eight to twelve.**

NONI'S RICOTTA PIE

Some of my favorite recipes come from my grandmother's family. Rich in heritage and flavor – and steeped in love – my Noni was actually ashamed to serve some of these remarkable recipes, for she considered them to be "peasant" food. The pie has evolved over the years but it still carries her legacy and her heart.

3 pounds Ricotta
1 pint heavy cream
½ cup flour
2 cups sugar
1 tablespoon vanilla
9 eggs
1 cup chocolate chips

Beat the eggs until thick. Add the sugar and beat well. Add the vanilla, cream and flour. Mix well. Fold in chocolate chips. Grease a baking dish well and pour the cheese mixture in. Bake at 350° for 1 ½ hours. **Serves eight.**

CHOCOLATE AVOCADO CAKE

3 cups cake flour
10 tablespoons unsweetened cocoa powder
½ teaspoon salt
2 teaspoons baking powder
2 teaspoons baking soda
2 cups granulated sugar
¼ cup butter
½ cup soft avocado (about 1 medium avocado) mashed until smooth and creamy
2 cups water
2 tablespoons white vinegar
2 teaspoons vanilla extract

FOR THE FROSTING:
8 ounces of avocado meat, about 2 small to medium, very ripe avocados
2 teaspoons lemon juice
1 pound powdered sugar, sifted
½ teaspoon vanilla extract
Shaved chocolate for garnish

Preheat oven to 350°. Spray a nine-inch cake round with Baker's Joy. Set aside. Sift together all of the dry ingredients. Mix all the wet ingredients together in a bowl, including the super mashed avocado. Mix the wet with the dry all at once, and beat with a whisk (by hand) until smooth. Pour batter into your prepared pan and bake for 40- 45 minutes, until a toothpick inserted comes out clean.

When the cake cooks, prepare the frosting. Peel and pit the soft avocados. Place the avocado meat into the bowl of a stand mixer fit with the whisk attachment. Add lemon juice and whisk the avocado on medium speed, until slightly lightened in color and smooth, about 2-3 minutes. Add the powdered sugar a little at a time and beat. Add vanilla extract until combined. If not using right away, store in the refrigerator (keep pit in the frosting so it does not turn brown). When ready to serve, frost completely and garnish with shaved chocolate. **Serves eight to twelve.**

STRAWBERRY MARGARITA PIE

Two months after I launched my gourmet mini pie business, my pie partner and I were discussing the upcoming Cinco de Mayo celebration, a big to do in Southern California. We renamed the holiday "Cinco de Pie-oh" and inspired by the day I created an alcohol free margarita pie. It remains our most popular flavor today and we offer it year round.

1 pint strawberries
2 tablespoons sugar
1 teaspoon orange zest, orange portion only
5 large egg yolks

One 14-ounce can sweetened condensed milk
½ cup fresh Key Lime juice (approximately 12 Key Limes)
2 teaspoons grated lime peel, green portion only

CRUST:
16 graham crackers
3 tablespoons sugar
1 cube butter

WHIPPING CREAM FOR GARNISH:
½ cup whipping cream
2 teaspoons granulated sugar
½ teaspoon vanilla
2 teaspoons grated lime peel, green portion only for garnish

Mix the pie crust ingredients and press them into a 9" pie plate. Bake in preheated 350° oven for 10-12 minutes until lightly browned.

Place strawberries, two tablespoons of sugar and the orange zest in a saucepan. Mix over low heat stirring constantly until soft, about 15 minutes. Let cool for a few minutes and blend with an emersions blender, leaving chunky. Use an electric mixer and beat the egg yolks until they are thick and turn to a light yellow. Don't over mix. Turn the mixer off and add the sweetened condensed milk. Turn speed to low and mix in half of the lime juice. Once the juice is incorporated add the other half of the juice and the zest, continue to mix until blended. Add the strawberry mixture and continue to mix until just blended, about one minute. Pour the mixture into the pie shell and bake at 350° for 12 minutes to set the yolks. Let cool completely.

Meanwhile in a clean bowl of an electric mixer beat the whipped cream, sugar and vanilla. Place in pastry bag with a star tip and pipe around the edges of the pie. If you don't have a pastry bag just dollop the cream decoratively around the edges. Sprinkle with grated lime zest and chill for at least two hours before serving. **Serves eight.**

SHIRLEY TEMPLE SCONES

For many, the introduction to sweet and savory came courtesy of the famed ginger, cherry, lemon & lime kiddie cocktail. I created this scone expressly for this recipe collection, and it's a tasty treat (brunch or dessert) for kids of all ages.

2 ¼ cups flour
⅓ cup sugar
1 tablespoon baking powder
1 teaspoon finely chopped lemon zest (about half the lemon)
1 teaspoon finely chopped lime zest (about one lime)
1 ½ sticks unsalted butter, grated and frozen for 15 minutes
½ cup candied ginger, finely chopped
1 cup assorted dried cherries
1 ½ cup heavy cream, plus extra for brushing the tops of the scones

In the bowl of a food processor combine the flour, sugar and baking powder and mix on low. Add the lemon and lime zest and butter and pulse until the mixture is a pale yellow and the consistency of fine meal. Transfer the mixture to a large bowl and stir in the ginger and the cherries. Make a well in the center and pour in the cream. Using one hand, draw in the dry ingredients, mixing until just combined.

Wash and dry your hands and dust them with flour. Turn the dough out onto a lightly floured work surface and gently knead a few times to gather it into a ball. Pat the dough into a circle about ¾ inches thick. Using a three-inch cookie cutter (or smaller if doing minis) cut out rounds. Gather the scraps, pat and press the pieces back together and cut out the remaining dough. Place the scones one inch apart on a parchment-lined baking sheet. Brush the tops with the remaining cream. Bake in a pre-heated 400° degree oven for 12 to 16 minutes, until they are pale browned. Let cool on rack before serving. **Makes one dozen.**

CHOCOLATE COVERED PRETZEL CHEESECAKE

My friend Wendy Lorenz shared an amazing cheesecake recipe with me, one she got from her mother JoJo. I made it for a party and was just about to serve it when a guest showed up with chocolate covered pretzels. I knew if I didn't somehow incorporate the pretzels into the dessert, I would eat every last one of them. I was inspired to top the already fabulous cheesecake with crumbled pretzels and it was even better than I could have imagined. I later tried it with chocolate covered peanut butter pretzels and it's a striking visual for parties and is absolutely delicious.

2 cups graham cracker crumbs
1 stick butter, melted
3 eight-ounce packages cream cheese
4 eggs, lightly beaten
½ cup sugar
1 cup 60% Cacao Bittersweet Chocolate Chips
1 teaspoon vanilla
2 cups chocolate covered pretzels, crumbled (you can buy them, or the recipe follows)

Preheat oven to 350°. Combine melted butter and crumbs. Press into a sprayed 9-inch spring form pan. In the bowl of an electric mixer beat the cream cheese. Add remaining ingredients and beat until smooth. Pour mixture into pan. Bake one hour and fifteen minutes, until firm in the middle. Remove from the oven and let cool for 15 minutes. Sprinkle the crumbled chocolate pretzels over the top of the cheesecake and press down a bit. Chill for a few hours (or overnight) before serving. Remove from the spring form pan and serve.

CHOCOLATE COVERED PRETZELS

10 ounces pretzel sticks or pretzel twists
12 ounces 60% Cacao Bittersweet Chocolate Chips

Melt chocolate chips in double broiler or in microwave (be careful not to burn in microwave). Carefully dip each pretzel in chocolate. Lay on wax paper lined baking sheets, lining up the rods leaving a bit of space between them so they're not touching. Let dry completely before crumbling. **Serves eight.**

COCKTAILS

I don't fancy myself a mixologist, and I am more of a wine girl than anything else. When my editor at My Daily Find ordered up a weekend cocktail column, I complied and had some fun with it. There are so many brilliant things you can bring into cocktails, just like food. And the sweet and savory combination was too tempting to resist. These recipes each serve two and should be made two at a time to maintain the integrity of the flavor. Cheers.

HOT CHERRY PEPPER MARTINI

3 ounces pepper infused vodka
6 drops grenadine
Juice of 1 lime
Fresh pitted cherries (preferred)
or maraschino cherries with stems attached

Combine vodka, grenadine, and lime juice in a cocktail shaker with ice. Strain into two chilled martini glasses and garnish three cherries.

JALAPEÑO MARGARITA

4 ounces jalapeño infused Tequila
4 ounces lime juice
4 ounces Cointreau

Rim two margarita glasses with salt. Shake vigorously and pour into prepared glasses.

PEAR AND ROSEMARY MARTINI

1 lemon or lime wedge
4 ounces pear juice
2 ounces pear vodka
1 ounce rosemary simple syrup
Sugar for rim of glass
Pear slices for garnish
Rosemary

Chill two martini glasses. Place sugar on a plate. Dampen the rim of the glass using the lemon wedge and dip into sugar to coat. In a cocktail shaker filled with ice, combine pear juice and vodka. Cover and shake. Strain into prepared glasses. Garnish with pear slices.

FRESH PEAR JUICE:
5 pears
3 cups water
½ cup granulated sugar
Juice of one large lemon

Select very ripe fruit. Peel and core pears. In a food processor crush pears. In a saucepan combine crushed pears with water and place on stove. Slowly heat to a simmer. Let cool down for a few minutes and press through a fine sieve. Add sugar and lemon juice bring to a light boil. Pour into a glass bottle and allow to cool.

ROSEMARY SIMPLE SYRUP:
16 sprigs rosemary
1 cup sugar
1 cup water

Heat sugar and water in a medium saucepan over medium-high heat, stirring until sugar has dissolved. Add rosemary; remove from heat. Let stand 30 minutes. Discard rosemary. Let cool completely. Syrup can be refrigerated in an airtight container up to 1 month.

GINGER INFUSED VODKA AND LEMONGRASS GREEN TEA

8 cups water
1 stalk lemongrass (half reserved for garnish)
10 thin slices of fresh ginger
7 bags green tea (white tea also works nicely)
2 cups ginger infused vodka

In a two quart saucepan place water, lemongrass and ginger. Bring to a rolling boil and remove from heat. Add teabags and let steep for 20 minutes. Remove teabags, lemongrass and ginger and let cool completely or overnight in the refrigerator. When ready to serve fill a large pitcher with ice and the vodka. Add the tea and mix well. Serve in glasses garnished with a lemongrass stalk.

GINGER SYRUP

1 lemon
2 cups coarsely chopped fresh ginger with peel, about 8 ounces
1 cup sugar
2 cups water

Remove the outer peel of the lemon with a vegetable peeler, taking care not to include too much of the bitter white pith. Finely chop the lemon peel and ginger in a food processor. Transfer the lemon-ginger mixture to a medium saucepan, add the sugar and water and bring to a boil. Reduce heat, and simmer, partially covered, for 15 minutes.

Strain the mixture and cool. Cover and refrigerate for up to two months. Makes approximately 2 cups.

APPLE GINGER MARTINI

6 ounces vodka
2 ounces ginger syrup
4 ounces apple juice
Two twists of lemon tossed in ¼ teaspoon cinnamon

Fill a cocktail shaker or small pitcher with ice. Add the vodka, ginger syrup, and apple juice. Cover and shake vigorously, or stir, until combined and chilled, about 30 seconds (in general, by the time the shaker mists up the drink is ready). Strain into two chilled martini glasses. Add cinnamon twist and serve.

GWEN'S SPA COCKTAIL

2 ounces vodka
2 ounces grapefruit juice
2 ounces lime juice
2 cans Sparkling Essence Cucumber
Mint for garnish

Fill two tall glasses with ice. Mix half the vodka, grapefruit juice and lime juice in each glass. Fill to the top of each glass with Sparkling Essence. Garnish with mint.

SALTY DOG

12 ounces grapefruit juice
3 ounces gin
Salt

Rim two tall glasses with salt and fill with crushed ice. Add the gin and grapefruit juice and stir well.

THE LAVENDER MARTINI

In a cocktail shaker filled with ice mix in:

4 ounces Absolute Citron or other lemon vodka
1 ounce Parfait Amor
1 ounce lavender infused simple syrup
½ ounce cranberry juice
1 lemon

Shake well.

Rim two martini glasses with equal parts of lemon & cranberry juice and place top of the glass on a flat plate with fine sugar, twist to cover the rim with sugar. Finish with a healthy squeeze of fresh lemon and a sprig of lavender.

LAVENDER SIMPLE SYRUP:
1 cup water
1 cup sugar
1 bunch lavender

In heavy medium saucepan over medium heat, stir together water and sugar until sugar dissolves. Increase heat slightly, and then simmer 5 minutes, stirring occasionally. Take pan off heat; add lavender and steep 30 minutes. Strain, and then refrigerate syrup until cold, about 3 hours.

CUCUMBER AND WATERMELON MOJITO

4 ounces rum
½ cup cucumber
½ cup watermelon
6 mint leaves
2 tablespoons agave nectar
1 ounce lime juice
Mint leaves and cucumber wheels for garnish

In a shaker muddle the mint leaves, watermelon and cucumbers. Add rum and agave nectar and shake well. Strain over fresh ice in two Collins glasses. Garnish with cucumber wheel and mint sprig.

THE MINT JULEP

2 ounces minted simple syrup
4-6 cups crushed ice
4 ounces bourbon
Fresh mint sprig, for garnish (spearmint is the official mint of the Derby)

Start with two highball glasses or two silver Julep cups then add minted simple syrup, then 1 cup crushed ice, bourbon, and splash of water. Fill the glasses to the top with ice and garnish with mint sprigs.

MINTED SIMPLE SYRUP:
1 cup water
1 cup sugar
1 bunch mint

In heavy medium saucepan over medium heat stir together water and sugar until sugar dissolves. Increase heat slightly and then simmer 5 minutes, stirring occasionally. Take pan off heat; add mint leaves and steep 15 minutes. Strain, and then refrigerate syrup until cold, about 3 hours.

ROSEMARY AND LEMON MARTINI

1 sprig fresh rosemary
1 ½ ounces vodka
½ ounce Limoncello
½ ounce fresh lemon juice
½ ounce simple syrup
1 rosemary sprig for garnish

Rim two martini glasses with rosemary sugar and set aside. Bend 1 rosemary sprig and drop into a cocktail shaker. Fill the shaker with ice. Add the vodka, Limoncello, lemon juice, and simple syrup. Cap and shake vigorously. Strain into the sugar-rimmed glass. Float a rosemary sprig in the drink for garnish.

ROSEMARY SUGAR:
2 tablespoons fresh rosemary leaves, coarsely chopped
1 cup superfine or Baker's sugar

Mix the rosemary and sugar together in a small bowl, and spread the mixture on a rimmed baking sheet. Set in a warm dry place for about four days, until the rosemary is completely dried. Process in a food processor or spice grinder until finely ground. Store in a tightly sealed container for up to one month at room temperature.

SIMPLE SYRUP:
1 cup granulated sugar
1 cup water

In a small saucepan heat the sugar and water and bring to a boil. When the sugar is completely dissolved remove from heat and cool to room temperature. Refrigerate, covered, for up to 1 week.

LIMONCELLO

25 lemons
2 (750-ml) bottle vodka
8 cups water
4 cups sugar

Using a vegetable peeler, remove the peel from the lemons in long strips (reserve the lemons for another use). Using a small sharp knife, trim away the white pith from the lemon peels; discard the pith. Place the lemon peels in a 2-quart pitcher. Pour the vodka over the peels and cover with plastic wrap. Steep the lemon peels in the vodka for seven days at room temperature.

After the seventh day stir the water and sugar in a large saucepan over medium heat until the sugar dissolves, about 5 minutes. Cool completely. Pour the sugar syrup over the vodka mixture. Cover and let stand at room temperature for 2 days. Strain the Limoncello through a mesh strainer. Discard the peels. Transfer the Limoncello to bottles. Seal the bottles and let set for at least 2 weeks.

KASTEL PUMPKIN PUNCH

Inspired by the trendy Kastel Lounge at Trump Soho.

5 ounces aged rum (they use Bacardi 8 Year Aged Rum)
2 ounces pineapple juice
½ ounce lemon juice
2 ounces orange juice
1 ounce spiced pumpkin puree
1 ounce date molasses
1 dash bitters (they use Fee's Original Bitters)
Nutmeg

Add all ingredients in a cocktail shaker filled with ice and shake vigorously. Serve in two burgundy glasses and garnish with nutmeg.

ACKNOWLEDGEMENTS

My mom Kay Kenneally who guides me here and my Dad, Jack Kenneally who guides me from the other side. My siblings, Elizabeth, Timothy, John and Mathew and my amazing nieces and nephews Alex, Katherine, Claire, Ryan, April, Katelyn and Matilda.

Emma, you delight me daily and I love the young woman you are becoming.

My girls (and guys) that are the best of friends who constantly inspire me and are so much fun to cook for and with: Linda, Wendy, Zeli, Dawn, Romy, ADM, Don, Steve, Dave and Marty.

My friends and family at The Agape International Spiritual Center. Rev. Michael, Rev. Kathleen, Rev. Rio, Rickie BB and my fellow practitioners. Thank you walking the journey with me!

A big shout out to the staff and crew at Back To The Kitchen Catering Company. Thank you for co-creating with me and always making me look so good. To my awesome clients: thank you for inviting me into your homes and allowing me to use your kitchens as my playground.

Karen Young - You had the daunting task of editing me to 750 words at the Sun and continue to do so this day at mydailyfind.com. You do it with such brilliance, grace and humor and I am by far a better writer because of you.

Judith Proffer - You saw a diamond in the rough (very rough) even before I could see it myself. You took a chef that tried to write recipes and molded me into a food writer. I am in constant awe of your grace, beauty and wisdom. I love you as a publisher, a partner in pie and mostly a cherished friend.

www.ingramcontent.com/pod-product-compliance
Lightning Source LLC
Chambersburg PA
CBHW042001150426
43194CB00002B/85